Song
Book

Play
Violin
Today!® Songbook

**Featuring 10
Rock & Pop
Favorites!**

ISBN 978-1-4234-9515-4

HAL•LEONARD®
CORPORATION

7777 W. BLUEMOUND RD. P.O. BOX 13819 MILWAUKEE, WI 53213

Visit Hal Leonard Online at
www.halleonard.com

Introduction

Welcome to the **Play Violin Today! Songbook**. This book includes 10 well-known rock and pop favorites, and is intended for the beginner to intermediate player.

The songs in this book are carefully coordinated with the skills introduced throughout the **Play Violin Today!** Method books 1 and 2. Refer to the right column in the table of contents below to see where each song fits within the method, and to help you determine when you're ready to play it.

Contents

About the CD

A full-band recording of each song in the book is included on the CD, so you can hear how it sounds and play along when you're ready. Each example is preceded by one or two measures of "clicks" to indicate the tempo and meter.

The CD is playable on any CD player, and is also enhanced so Mac and PC users can adjust the recording to any tempo without changing the pitch!

Track 1

My Heart Will Go On
(Love Theme from 'Titanic')
from the Paramount and Twentieth Century Fox Motion Picture TITANIC

VIOLIN

Music by JAMES HORNER
Lyric by WILL JENNINGS

Count 8 measures of whole rests.

Track 2

How to Save a Life

VIOLIN

Words and Music by JOSEPH KING
and ISAAC SLADE

Can You Feel the Love Tonight

from Walt Disney Pictures' THE LION KING

Track 3

VIOLIN

Music by ELTON JOHN
Lyrics by TIM RICE

Fields of Gold

Track 4

VIOLIN

Music and Lyrics by
STING

Lean on Me

Track 5

VIOLIN

Words and Music by
BILL WITHERS

Track 6

A Time for Us
(Love Theme)
from the Paramount Picture ROMEO AND JULIET

VIOLIN

Words by LARRY KUSIK and EDDIE SNYDER
Music by NINO ROTA

Slowly and expressively

rit. (2nd time)

Sunrise, Sunset

from the Musical FIDDLER ON THE ROOF

Track 7

Words by SHELDON HARNICK
Music by JERRY BOCK

VIOLIN

Moderately slow Waltz tempo

In My Life

Track 8

VIOLIN

Words and Music by JOHN LENNON
and PAUL McCARTNEY

Track 9

Salty Dog Blues

VIOLIN

Words and Music by WILEY A. MORRIS
and ZEKE MORRIS

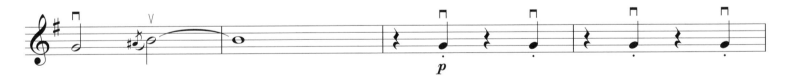

Somewhere Out There

from AN AMERICAN TAIL

Track 10

VIOLIN

Music by BARRY MANN and JAMES HORNER
Lyric by CYNTHIA WEIL

Moderately, with expresson

electric piano

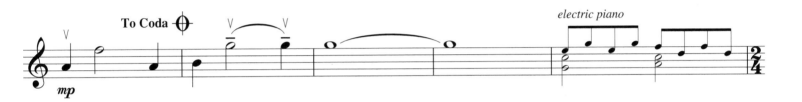

Fingering Charts

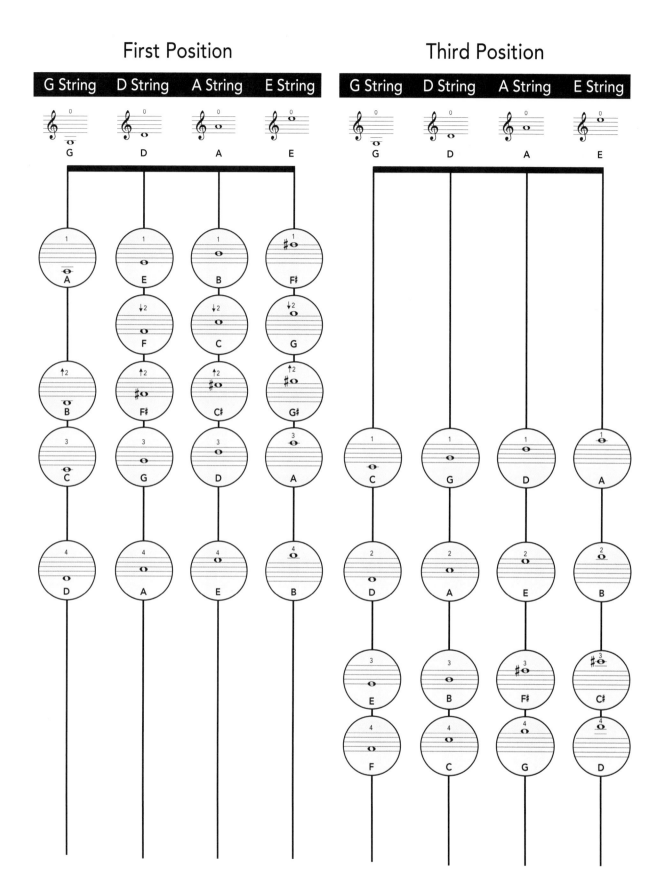

First Position

Third Position